Can I Trust You?

67+1 Habits that will make you a trustworthy team member

Yoram Solomon, PhD

Innovation
Culture
Institute

To all team members who had my back and to all veterans. Thank you for your service.

Can I Trust You?

67+1 Habits that will make you a trustworthy team member

Table of Contents

Foreword

In March 2015, I ran a campaign to be elected to the Plano Independent School District board. Plano ISD is one of the most prominent, strongest school districts in the nation. Part of campaigning was meeting with potential supporters. In one of those meetings, over breakfast, one potential supporter told me that he had asked about me and was given the feedback about a concern with me not being a "team player."

As much as I tried to hide my feelings, I was hurt. But then I realized that the definition of **team player** is different in different places and for different people. On the board or council of an elected government entity, being a team player often means that you are expected to go along with the majority, and any sign of disagreement on the board is considered negative.

But I was hurt for another reason. You see, I served in the Israeli Defense Forces 35th Airborne Brigade as an infantry soldier, operating high-power weapons in extremely adverse situations. I was part of a team, in which my team members trusted me with their lives, and I trusted them with mine. That was our definition of being a team-player.

It hurt my feelings that the impression was that I wasn't.

This book is the third in a series of mini books that are based on original research I have conducted, starting with my 2010 doctoral dissertation that focused on understanding the differences in corporate culture between startups and mature companies. The research I conducted over the past decade led to the creation of the **Innovation Culture Institute LLC**.

The book is also based on hundreds of articles I published over the years in publications such as **Inc.** Magazine, Innovation Excellence, Directors & Boards, and many more.

Finally, it is also based on my experience in building trust through different roles and disciplines, from being an executive in several private and public companies, to helping other organizations, from startups to Fortune 500 companies, build their own culture of innovation and trust.

But it is important to note that I learned the most about trust not by reading books or conducting research.

There are different levels of **trust** and **trustworthiness**. There is the level of trustworthiness you must possess if you expect me to trust you to return a $20 bill that I lent you. There is a different level of trustworthiness you must have if you expect me to give you my email password to check my emails. There is yet a higher level of trustworthiness you must have if you expect me to trust you, as a surgeon, to operate on my daughter.

I learned about trust as an infantry soldier and marksman at the Israeli Defense Forces 35th Airborne Paratroopers Brigade.

Finally, I learned the most about **trust** when I trusted my platoon members with my life. I learned about **trustworthiness** when I asked my platoon members to trust me with theirs.

Nevertheless, I will not claim that I'm a great team member. Not even that I'm a good one. I will claim, though, that based on my research and experience, I know what makes a **trustworthy team member**, and that's what I'll share with you here.

Enjoy the book,

Why is it so important to be a trustworthy team member?

When I conducted my doctoral research in 2008-2010, I discovered that a creative and productive organizational culture exists only when **team dynamics** are positive. Through the research I found that positive team dynamics boil down to one element: the ability to **disagree constructively**.

In my study (and beyond), I observed three types of disagreements: the politically correct disagreement, the constructive disagreement, and the destructive disagreement.

The politically correct disagreement focuses on avoiding disagreement altogether. People hold the meeting **before** the meeting, the meeting **after** the meeting, just not the meeting **during** the meeting.

The destructive disagreement quickly turns personal, emotional, and irrational. It is not about ideas anymore. It's about personalities. It's not that your idea is stupid. **You** are stupid!

Needless to say (or maybe it is needed?) that neither of these two types of disagreement are productive and will contribute to the organization's success.

In 2018, I conducted another study, correlating the ability (and willingness) to hold **constructive disagreement** to the level of **trust** in the team.

My findings confirmed what I suspected. In high-trust teams, 94% of the members reported that they could disagree without letting it become personal, or even passionately disagree while remaining friends. Only 6% of them reported that disagreements were unproductive, that they didn't feel comfortable disagreeing, or that they tried to avoid disagreements altogether. In a low-trust team, 61% of the members reported those negative feelings. Ten times more than in a high-trust team!

As I analyzed the elements that allowed teams to hold constructive disagreements, I found three:

- The willingness to be **vulnerable** with one another, ask stupid questions, and suggest stupid ideas
- The willingness to provide direct and honest **feedback**
- The **receptivity** to such feedback.

Therefore, not surprisingly, I found that the willingness to be vulnerable was 240% higher, the willingness to provide direct feedback was 106% higher, and the receptivity to such feedback was 76% higher in high-trust teams than in low-trust teams.

Later that year, I conducted another study. Initially, as an open-ended question, I asked the participants what the most important quality for them in other people was. I then took the top five qualities and asked the same question in a quantitative survey. This time, I was more specific. I asked participants about the most important quality in six types of people / roles:

- Their bosses
- Their employees
- Their colleagues / peers
- A salesperson trying to sell them something
- Their government representatives
- Their spouses

Based on the initial open-ended pilot study, I gave them five options to choose from:

- Willingness to work hard
- Willingness to take risk
- Intelligence
- Trustworthiness
- Good looks

I know, good looks was one of the top options. Thankfully, only 0.83% of the participants ranked good looks as the most important quality for them in other people...

Alarmingly, 0.83% of people ranked good looks as the most important quality for them in other people!!!

But that's a topic for another book.

Trustworthiness was the highest ranked quality, with 61.2% of participants ranking trustworthiness as the most important quality for them in other people, across all roles, compared to 38.8% for the other four qualities combined.

However, those results were less decisive when I isolated what participants told me about their teammates. While still in top place, only 49.2% of participants ranked trustworthiness of their peers as the most important quality, followed by 33.9% for willingness to work hard (compared to the 30.1% workplace average and 19.8% overall). In other words, less than half of the participants ranked trustworthiness as the most important quality in other people.

It was definitely worse when I asked **leaders** about their **employees**. When asking leaders what the most important quality for them in their employees was, they ranked the

willingness to work hard as the most important quality, 47.5% of the time. Trustworthiness only came second, 39.3% of the time. But that's the topic of another book: *Can I TRUST You? 70+1 Habits that will make you a trustworthy* **Leader**.

In this book, I will focus on the team itself and how to become a more trustworthy team member, as viewed by your peers.

With that, let me offer you 67+1 habits that will help you become a trustworthy **team member**.

Does that sound like a plan?

What is Trust, Anyway?

But before I can start, I must first define a few things. To me, the definition of trust is the following:

> **The level to which you are willing to accept the potential negative consequences of giving control over something you have to another person.**

This means different things in different contexts. In the context of teamwork, each team member has control over their careers and their ability to earn money. They are willing to let you, their teammate, be the determining factor of how much they enjoy their job, and how much you can affect their success in (and compensation from) it. The potential negative consequences to your teammates of giving you control over those, most times, are that they could lose their job, earn less (if the team is not successful), or lose their enjoyment in it.

Their willingness to accept those potential negative consequences is the level by which they trust you.

There are seven laws you must know about trust:

1. *Trust is a range*. It is not a binary yes/no variable. There is no "I trust you" or "I don't trust you." There is only "how much I trust you."
2. *Trust is contextual*. You may be trusted more to do one thing (return my money), and less to do something else (perform surgery).
3. *Trust exists independently between two people*, at different degrees. There is no such thing as the overall trust level of a team. It is made of the individual trust levels between every two members of the team.
4. *Trust is a two-way street, but not a symmetrical one*. You may trust someone, but they may not trust you at the same level (they could trust you more or less).
5. *Trust has two sides*. The level of trust one person has in another is the product of the first person's trustability (willingness to trust others in general) and the trustworthiness of the second person.
6. *Trust and Trustworthiness are reciprocal and circular*. If one person is trustworthy, the other tends to trust him/her. If one person trusts another, the other tends to rise to the occasion and be more trustworthy.
7. *Trust is transferrable*. If person **A** trusts person **B**, and person **B** trusts person **C**, then person **A** may trust person **C**, although to a lesser degree that the first two trust relationships.

The Trustactions™ Model

After years of research, I developed the following model. I found that this model applies to **every** relationship. In this book, I applied it to the **team / collegial / peer** relationship.

I like to look at trust as a cycle. Your trustworthiness may cause a teammate to trust you, which will reinforce your trustworthiness (especially since you quickly realize that your trustworthiness leads to a better willingness / ability to hold constructive disagreement, which leads to better productivity, creativity, success, and overall job satisfaction). On the other hand, your untrustworthiness may cause your teammate to distrust you, which will only reinforce your untrustworthiness.

As a result, you will typically operate in either cycle with any teammate. Most likely, you will be in the same cycle with **all** of your teammates.

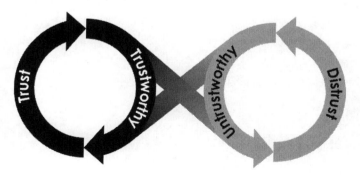

However, there is a way to break out of a cycle. Your teammate may distrust you initially, but you can break out of the distrust cycle, by demonstrating trustworthy actions that will change your teammate's perception of you and move that relationship into the trust cycle. In this book, I will teach you 67 habits that will help you get there and stay there.

Unfortunately, your teammate may begin by trusting you, yet your untrustworthy actions will cause them to distrust you. Don't do that. Follow the advice in this book. Learn and practice the habits described in it.

Building trust happens during every interaction with every teammate, but also before and after those interactions.

I call the factors that build (or destroy) trust during an interaction **transactional** factors, and those that take place outside of an interaction **contextual** factors. There are three factors in each category. Each one of them has the potential to build, or destroy, trust.

CONTEXTUAL

Competence

Shared Values

Fairness / Symmetry

TRANSACTIONAL

Time

Intimacy

Positivity

The *contextual* factors include **competence**, **shared values**, and **fairness** (or **symmetry**).

Competence is the extent to which your teammates believe that you know your job as part of the team, and that you are good at it. It is contextual because your teammates don't care how well you play golf. Typically...

Shared values are the extent to which your teammates believe you have their best interest in mind because you are like them, and therefore you value the same things. Some values are universal, some are individual (personality types, for example), and some are inter-personal and unique to the combination of you and any specific teammate.

Fairness / Symmetry is the extent to which you are equal in your relationship. Your teammates need to feel that your relationship is based on fairness and symmetry, and that both of you have something to gain from the successful outcome, and you both have something to lose if the outcome is not successful. Fairness and Symmetry may occur in other areas than compensation or office size to still matter.

The **_transactional_** elements occur during every interaction between you and your teammate, and include **time**, **intimacy**, and **positivity**.

Time, simply put, is the amount of time you and your teammate spend together interacting. The more time you spend together, the more opportunity you have to gain their trust. A significant component of the time factor is the **first impression**. Not all time has the same impact on building trust. You don't get a second chance to make a first impression. The first impression you make has the highest impact on your trustworthiness.

Intimacy is the level of interaction you have, where text messages and email are at the lowest end of the spectrum, phone calls above it, and face-to-face meetings at the top, or close to it. Intimacy can be associated with Albert Mehrabian's 7-38-55 rule (7% of likeability is attributed to the **words** you use, 38% to your **tone** of voice, and 55% to your **body language**).

Positivity is *not* referring to the positivity of the *situation* you are in, but rather to your teammate's view of the positivity of *your behavior* during the interaction with them. Once you left the meeting, did your employees have a positive or negative impression of you (specifically, your competence, shared values, and fairness)?

Finally, I wanted to share the Trustactions™ **formula** set that I developed at the Innovation Culture Institute over the past few years, which explains how trust develops.

Explaining this formula set, how it evolved, and what each part of it means is beyond the scope of this book, but I wanted you to just get a glimpse at it and realize that such a formula set exists.

$$T_t = \sqrt[3]{C_t V_t F_t}$$

$$C_t = C_0 + \sum_{i=1}^{i=t} t_i \left(\beta + \frac{(1-\beta)t_i}{\sum_{j=1}^{j=i} t_j} \right) i_i \left(\frac{\delta+1}{2} \Delta pC_i - \frac{\delta-1}{2} |\Delta pC_i| \right)$$

$$V_t = V_0 + \sum_{i=1}^{i=t} t_i \left(\beta + \frac{(1-\beta)t_i}{\sum_{j=1}^{j=i} t_j} \right) i_i \left(\frac{\delta+1}{2} \Delta pV_i - \frac{\delta-1}{2} |\Delta pV_i| \right)$$

$$F_t = F_0 + \sum_{i=1}^{i=t} t_i \left(\beta + \frac{(1-\beta)t_i}{\sum_{j=1}^{j=i} t_j} \right) i_i \left(\frac{\delta+1}{2} \Delta pF_i - \frac{\delta-1}{2} |\Delta pF_i| \right)$$

As much as it would be nice and clear (great for my OCD), each of the following 67 habits does not squarely fit in only one of the six Trustactions™ categories. These habits cut across them, and I've put each one under only one category to eliminate redundancy.

Habit #1: Competence

Be good at what you do

Your teammates expect you to know what you are doing as a part of the team. They expect you to have their backs in your area of expertise. They will perceive you as someone who knows what he/she is doing through:

- Your level of **education**, specifically in the technical skills relevant to your role. Even the schools you went to will count towards validating your educational competence.
- Your **experience**, in terms of the companies you worked for (are those admired by your teammates?), your past performance, and the areas you have worked in.
- Your **brand**. The best definition I've ever heard for the word brand is: *what people say about you when you're not in the room.* Your teammates will hear about you from other people. Most likely other people who have worked with you. What will those former colleagues say about you?

Know what other team members are doing

Yes, you have a well-defined role within the team.

No, you don't have the skills or the time to do the others' jobs.

No, they don't want you to do their jobs.

But they do expect you to know what they are working on, what challenges they have, and to sometimes be a sounding board to them.

Spend time learning what they are working on, by asking them. Don't surprise them with an unexpected depth of knowledge you have about their jobs.

The fact that you know enough about their challenges and efforts to have empathy for them will gain you credibility with them.

Habit #3: Competence

Do what you say

There is almost no faster way to lose credibility, perception of competence, and trustworthiness than not doing what you said you will do.

Competence (or trust) doesn't mean that you must agree with another person on everything. You may have a differing opinion on things, even on technical things that might seemingly not be open to interpretation.

But your consistency and the fact that you do what you said contributes more to your competence and trustworthiness than your technical know-how.

When you promise to do something, put it on your calendar. If you are a procrastinator you will put it on the due date. If you like to get things done early—you will put it there earlier. Just make sure you do what you said.

Habit #4: Competence

Watch your social media footprint

Your teammates will look you up on social media. Trust me. They may not ask you for your friendship through social media, but they will look you up, and will continue to do this on a regular basis.

What does your social media footprint say about you?

You may think that you are separating your private life from your professional life, but guess what? I can still see your Facebook posts. Even if I'm not your friend on Facebook.

You may decide to keep your privacy, and you are certainly entitled to do that. However, transparency plays a big role in your team's perception of you.

Make sure that your social media footprint represents the person that your teammates see at work. The person you want them to see.

Habit #5: Competence

Give autonomy

The word autonomy is perceived to be associated with leadership rather than teamwork. In fact, it exists in both.

Teresa Amabile's definition of autonomy is my favorite: It is not letting someone decide **which** mountain to climb, but rather letting them decide **how** to climb it.

When you are not the team leader, you don't really determine which mountain to climb.

However, in an effective and productive team, team members keep each other accountable.

You need to find the fine line between keeping a teammate accountable for their job and micro-managing their job.

Watch the detail level and frequency of checking up on your teammates. Don't overdo it.

Habit #6: Competence

"Her confidence"

In the movie *Zero Dark Thirty*, one navy SEAL wonders why his teammate is convinced that their HVT (High Value Target) was Bin-Laden. "What part convinced you?" the SEAL asked, to which his teammate pointed to Maya, the CIA agent, and replied: "her confidence".

Your confidence is like transferrable trust. It's convincing others that you trust yourself.

Your confidence as a team member in what you do for the team and in the direction the team is going in is critical to your teammates' perception of your competence.

Any cracks in your confidence will show. Even if you try to hide them. Especially if you try to hide them (see *Watch your tone and body language* later in the book).

Don't confuse confidence with arrogance, recklessness, or blind passion. Those will achieve the opposite result.

Habit #7: Competence

Love what you do

You cannot expect your team members to do their respective parts in a team project and be competent doing so if they don't **love** what they do.

The same applies to you. If you don't love what you do, your teammates will notice that, and will not think you are competent.

Remember that they are more influenced by your body language than by your words, while you are less consciously in control of your body language than of your words.

So, if you don't **love** what you do—stop doing that. You (and your team members) are better off having another member doing what you're supposed to do, someone who truly loves doing it (and therefore perceived as competent).

Spare them the agony.

Habit #8: Competence

Commit to self-develop

You may have the right education, background, and experience. You may also show that you love what you do, but your knowledge and experience have expiration dates on them.

Knowing what was known in your industry domain and skill group 20 years ago doesn't show commitment to remaining competent.

Make sure you continue to self-improve.

You must do that at the technical domain (e.g., artificial intelligence, family law, retail packaging). You should know the latest developments in your field.

But you must also do that at the technical skill you are using that makes you good. Learn the latest techniques, tools, and disciplines.

Show your teammates you are committed to stay competent.

Habit #9: Competence

Develop others

Not only you should continue to develop yourself, you must also actively participate in developing others in the organization.

When you teach others, you learn more yourself. Every time my daughter needed to prepare for a test in high school, she would ask me to be her student, and would teach me what she had just learned.

Teaching helps you study. The questions you may get from your teammates who sit through your lessons help you improve and deepen your own knowledge.

But also, when you teach others, they consider you more competent in what you do.

Developing others also increases the perception of shared values (you show that you care for the development of others) and fairness/symmetry (you are not afraid of them knowing as much as you do).

Habit #10: Shared Values

Celebrate success

In my research, I found that team members gave the highest importance to the recognition they get from their **peers**, followed by the recognition from their **immediate leader**, and only last—the recognition by top management (such as the company's **CEO**). You would think they would appreciate the CEO's recognition the most, but they don't.

Make sure you recognize your teammates' successes. But don't fake it. Be genuine. Show them that you share their success. Don't celebrate trivial things as if they were significant. That's fake.

Don't pass the opportunity to recognize significant achievements. If you recognize the smallest milestones, you would have overused that card. But if you don't recognize the major achievements, you would come across as taking them (teammates and achievements) for granted, or simply don't care.

Habit #11: Shared Values

Accept, but don't celebrate failure

New management approaches emphasize accepting failure. I agree with that. However, I've seen companies take failure acceptance to the extreme. They celebrated failure as if it was the goal.

When you do that, the line between success and failure starts to blur. It is not clear anymore what the desired outcome is.

Treat failure as an unavoidable part of life. Treat it as something that happens naturally on the path to success, but don't treat it as success. It will confuse the team.

After a teammate reported failure, give them feedback (when appropriate). Don't beat your teammate down. But they shouldn't feel like winners, either.

You should be able to give them ideas. Possibly hold a constructive failure analysis session to learn from that failure, but never celebrate it.

Habit #12: Shared Values

Identify the common enemy

One of the strongest elements of shared values is the existence of a common enemy. The enemy can, but doesn't have to be a **person**.

It could be the fear of not having enough money to put your kids through college. It could be a fear of your car breaking down.

It could be any one of many possible things that both you and your teammates are afraid of, ashamed of, worried about, or simply hate (not a word I like to use often).

A common enemy could even be a football team or a bad referee call during the Super Bowl, as long as you both feel the same.

Identify an enemy you have in common with your teammates and let them know. You will immediately elevate the level of shared values they feel they have with you. Sharing a fear of something bad is stronger than sharing a love for something good.

Habit #13: Shared Values

Tell the truth

Do you like it when someone lies to your face, knowingly and intentionally, while trying to hide it? I didn't think so. I don't even know you and I still know this about you.

The truth is one of those universal values that is true for everyone (no pun intended). One of the great things about telling the truth is that you never have to remember what you said and to whom.

There are also many signs that you are lying. Did you know that when you look up and to the right, many psychologists believe that it is a sign that you are lying (getting in touch with your "creative side of the brain")?

We can sense (often, although not always) when people lie to us.

Don't lie. Tell the truth. It's an important universal shared value that would increase your trustworthiness. Lying would destroy it.

Habit #14: Shared Values

Be an open book

Your teammates will not be able to know that you share their values if they know nothing about you. Yes, the workplace is a professional environment, and it's up to you to decide how much personal "stuff" you want to disclose.

The more you share with your teammates, the more they get to know you, the more they get to see that you are human, and the more they can relate to you and feel they share values with you.

Two of the most important things you should share with your teammates are your **values** and **beliefs**. Your values are what drive your decisions and actions. If they know your values, they will better understand **why** you do what you do.

Share not only what your values are, but also how you made decisions. This will help reduce the uncertainty of working with you.

Habit #15: Shared Values

Explain why

Suppose you are telling your team that you are about to do something (related to the team's goals), or asking someone on the team to do something. Your teammate may be asking you "why?"

"Because I know what I'm doing (or why I'm asking for it)" is not a good answer.

Yes, you might know something that they don't. Most likely you do. However, not sharing it reduces your trustworthiness.

You don't have to provide the smallest of details, but explaining why you are doing something (or asking them to do something) shares the bigger picture with them.

Don't put trust to the test if you don't have to. After a while, they will stop asking "why" because they trust you. But if someone is asking—tell them why.

Habit #16: Shared Values

Be predictable

In general, people like predictability and don't like surprises.

Your team members don't like you to be unpredictable. Their job is probably stressful even without you being unpredictable.

Don't add unpredictability.

Try to make their work, and specifically working with *you*, as predictable as possible. This way, you would make them feel more comfortable and know that you can be relied upon, that you will deliver what's expected of you, that you have their back, and thus you share their values.

And they will consider you more trustworthy for that.

Be predictable.

Habit #17: Shared Values

Don't expect, ask!

Do you sometimes expect something from one of your colleagues, just to be disappointed later when they don't deliver it, even though you never specifically asked for it?

You're not alone. We all do it. We expect other people (in this case, your teammates) to read our minds. We believe that we gave clear enough **clues** to what we were expecting. So much so that we don't really have to say the actual words.

"Do you really need me to spell it out for you?" is what we think, and sometimes what we say.

But the bottom line is that we do need to spell it out. You have to tell your teammates what you are asking of them, and be very clear and specific about it. Don't expect them to read your mind, or read between the lines. Maybe they can't. That's **your** fault. Not theirs.

Habit #18: Shared Values

What do we have in common?

Imagine being on a trip to a foreign country, far away from home. You don't really understand or speak the language. Suddenly, you hear someone speaking English. What do you feel? You reach out to that person and ask them where they are from. They tell you they are from the U.S. What does that make you feel? They are from your home state, your home town, and went to the same high-school as you. What do you feel about them now?

There is a lot of power in having things in common. Research your teammates (LinkedIn, Facebook, through common connections), focus on the things you have in common. Let your teammates know what you have in common with them. "Did you know we went to the same college?"

Identifying those shared experiences will increase your contextual trustworthiness.

Habit #19: Shared Values

Know what you don't have in common

At the same time, watch for things you **don't** have in common, and specifically where you are on opposite sides of issues.

I'm not a proponent of bringing political or controversial issues to a business meeting. Those have more potential to cause harm than do good.

You're a Republican and your teammate, as observed in her Facebook page, is a Democrat. How well do you think this will go if you bring up politics? You may be a Dallas Cowboys fan while your teammate is a Patriots fan. How well do you think that would go?

Just as much as you want to identify the values you have in common and bring them into the conversation to build trust, know what you don't have in common and do your best to avoid those topics. At least until you have trust.

Habit #20: Shared Values

Don't assume, ask!

I remember my first boss in the U.S., the CEO of Voyager Technologies, who told me that "when you **assume**, you make an **ass** out of **u** and **me**..." Did you get that?

You make assumptions about your teammates. Sometimes those assumptions are based on homework you did before. Sometimes you make assumptions because of the way they look, the way they talk, or what their home / car / clothes / watch / pen look like.

And as good as your gut feeling is, you may be wrong.

Ask yourself what do you really know for a *fact*, and what you are *assuming* about your teammate.

Don't make assumptions. Ask questions instead. Only then act on what you *know* to be true, and not what you assume.

Habit #21: Shared Values

Don't badmouth others

Nobody is perfect. Neither are you. How often do you find flaws in other people? How often do you find flaws in other teammates of yours (current and past)? And more important— when you find those flaws—do you share them with others?

You may be having a private conversation with a teammate. During that conversation, you may say that you are displeased with another member of the team, or even someone outside the team.

Your teammate might even feel the same, but deep inside they will be wondering if you speak negatively about them behind their backs, too.

It doesn't matter that you and your teammate share the same negative feelings about another person. Don't speak negatively about someone else with your teammate.

Habit #22: Shared Values

Avoid BCC

Imagine this. A teammate had just sent you an email. Your email address was the only one in the **To** field. There was nothing in the **CC** field. However, an hour later, your boss replied to this email. How could that be?

Because your boss was **BCC**'d.

If you look up the definition of BCC (Blind Carbon Copy), you will find that it's a "useful way to let others see an e-mail you sent without the main recipient knowing."

So, what do you feel when you realize that your teammate emailed you something and copied your boss **with the intention of you not knowing**? How is *that* for shared values? By the way, it doesn't even matter if this was not their intention.

Congratulations! You just learned why you should never use BCC when you email a teammate.

Habit #23: Fairness / Symmetry

What happened one inch outside the frame never happened

Once, a colleague complained to me that while he was doing good things that others didn't know about, they were complaining that he wasn't doing enough.

I thought about an analogy from the field of photography. When you see the inside of a video studio, it's a mess of lights, microphones, wires, and all kinds of devices around the subject. However, when the camera is zoomed on the subject, none of those show. The image in the camera's frame is clean and uncluttered.

"What happens one inch outside of the frame never happened," I told him.

I'm not suggesting you do everything for show, but if your teammates don't know what you are doing, they might believe that you are not "pulling your own weight" in the team.

Habit #24: Fairness / Symmetry

Put as much effort

Your team (and therefore you), might be in a time-crunch. You might be under a lot of pressure to meet a deadline. Your team members may work 10, 12, 16, or more hours per day (by the way, the number of hours per day doesn't have to be even...). They might be working at night and over weekends.

Even if your part of the overall team effort is lighter, or even done, do your best to be there with them. They need to see that you work as hard as they do.

When you're with them, if you don't have anything to do for your own part of the task, and you can help them in what they do, great! They might not want you to, and you might not be able to. That's fine. Still, don't let them feel that they are working harder than you are.

Habit #25: Fairness / Symmetry

Start with trust

Remember the 4th and 6th laws of trust? Trust between two people is a two-way street, albeit not a symmetrical one, and trust and trustworthiness have a reciprocal relationship.

It is *your* decision whether to trust a new team member **before** they earned your trust.

You can decide not to trust them until they earned your trust. But, guess what? If you don't trust them, it will become a self-fulfilling prophecy, and they will justify your lack of trust by not acting in a trustworthy way towards you.

And if you don't trust them, even if not in a completely symmetrical way, they won't trust you.

But if you **do** trust them before they earned your trust, they will justify your trust in them by being trustworthy, and they will trust you back.

Habit #26: Fairness / Symmetry

Offer to help

If you bury your head in your task you may come across as competent and dedicated, but not caring that your teammates might be struggling with their tasks.

Get your head "above water" and check in with your teammates. Do they need any help? Is there anything you can do to help them?

Offer to help. It might be a low-skill task that might help them get ahead.

When you offer, fully expect to be taken up on your offer and be ready to help them.

After all, it doesn't matter if you finished your task on time, on budget, and on specification if others on your team didn't. What matters is the overall goal given to the team. Helping everyone finish their tasks on time is a strong sign of fairness and symmetry.

Habit #27: Fairness / Symmetry

Ask for help

The more you come across as someone who knows everything and doesn't need any help, the less symmetrical your relationships with your teammates are, and the less trustworthy you are perceived to be by them.

Recognize that you could use their help. Ask for their help. This is nothing to be ashamed of. You will only show your teammates that you are human. You will acknowledge that you don't know everything. You will acknowledge that, God forbid, there are things that they know and that you don't!

It will show them that you respect their knowledge, experience, and skills.

They will feel good about helping you.

And it will allow them to feel more comfortable asking for help themselves. From you, or from others.

Say "Thank you"

If someone helped you with part of your task, don't take it for granted. Sure, they may have helped you just to make sure the overall team task is finished on time, or because someone asked them to help you.

Nevertheless, they did help you.

A symmetrical relationship is not limited to "favors" going in both directions equally. It can also be the appreciation you show for a favor coming your way.

Be genuine when you thank your teammate for helping.

You may not even need their help, but still thank them for offering to help. This will also assure that they will offer again.

Habit #29: Fairness / Symmetry

Don't ask of others what you don't demand of yourself

This is one of the fundamental rules of symmetry and fairness in a working relationship.

Having said that, it is one of the hardest one to do. Imagine this. You are driving and you see someone in the car next to you texting while driving. "How irresponsible and dangerous!" you think to yourself. Not five minutes later, your phone indicates that you got a text. Quickly (and carefully, of course) you look at that text. Why do those rules apply to the other drivers but not to you?

If you frown at someone who came late to a meeting, don't be late to meetings yourself. If you don't like when a teammate takes a call during a meeting—don't take calls yourself.

Don't hold your teammates to a higher standard than the one you are willing to hold yourself to.

Habit #30: Fairness / Symmetry

Be critical, not judgmental

The dictionary definitions of the two words are somewhat intertwined and, frankly, not very helpful.

So, let me give you my definition, focusing on the difference between the two words.

Being judgmental is **backward**-looking. You approve (or disapprove) of something your teammate has done. You measured *their* actions (or results) against *your* standards.

Being critical is both backward- and **forward**-looking. You render an opinion on something your teammate has done, but with the context of how it could be done better in the future.

Add one word: **because**. What you did was [select: good | bad] because...

Explain what was wrong in the context of the consequences, and how it could be better.

Be critical, not judgmental.

Habit #31: Time

Be on time

There is a saying that "early is on time, on time is late, and late is unacceptable." Do you always show up on time?

Maybe you don't, but the others on your team do. What if your teammates don't care if you are late, yet you show up on time to a meeting with them? Do you have anything to lose? Will they think less of you? No.

But what if your teammates really care if you are on time (just like me...), yet you are consistently late?

Be on time to meetings with your teammates. Don't be late. Being late may increase asymmetry in your relationships.

And remember, being on time (or late) is the first impression you leave on your teammates. It's how you start the meeting. Later in this book I will explain the importance of the first impression to your trustworthiness.

Be available for your teammates

You are busy. I get that. Your teammates are busy as well. But when one of them needs you, do your best to make yourself available, whether this is a technical, work-related, or personal issue.

This may not be a critical or even important issue for you, but it might be important or even critical to them. The more important it is to them, the more you should drop everything to listen to them, and help if you can.

This might not be an important thing, even for them. They may just not realize that you are a little too busy right now, or in the middle of something that you can't stop. In that case, tell them and schedule a time, soon, to have the conversation. The ball will not be in your court.

But if you availed yourself to them, be present. Don't use your phone, computer, or do other work.

Habit #33: Time

Respect other people's time

You may have some free time on your hands, but that doesn't mean that your team members do as well.

I saw team members talk with other team members possibly about work-related things, but sometimes about unimportant things (at least, not important to their teammates), completely ignoring how busy their teammates are at the time.

If you are going to interrupt what your teammate is working on, do it only if it's really urgent, or if you think that he or she may stop what they are doing or do it differently based on what you are about to tell them (such as when a fundamental assumption they are using to do their work had changed).

Even then, don't assume you can just barge in whenever it is convenient for you. Respect their time.

Habit #34: Time

Follow up

The amount of time required to build trust is not only the time you spend *in the meeting* with your teammates. It is also the frequency of your follow-up after and between meetings.

First, if you promised to follow up in two weeks, do exactly that. Especially if your team members' tasks depend on something they need from you.

If you promised to follow up in two weeks but took three weeks to do so, you would be perceived as not taking their concerns seriously enough, and not keeping your word.

If you promised to follow up in two weeks yet followed up in only one week, you may be putting too much pressure and, believe it or not, would still not be keeping your word.

But if you follow up exactly when you said you would, you just earned a few points of trustworthiness.

Spend time with each team member

The more time you spend with each team member individually, the more you get to know them, the more they get to know you, and the more they get to **trust** you (presuming that you can establish competence, shared values, and fairness when you spend time with them).

Don't assume that spending an hour in a meeting with six members of your team is the same as spending an hour with each one of them individually.

During a one-on-one meeting with a teammate, both of you can be more open and vulnerable with each other more than when there are five other people present.

This would also be the ideal time to provide feedback, instead of during a meeting with five other team members.

First impression

We remember the first impression with another person more than other interactions with them.

A study conducted by Microsoft found that the average human attention span dropped from 12 seconds in 2000 to 8 seconds in 2013.

In *Blink*, author Malcolm Gladwell claimed that we learn much more in the first 15 minutes than we do in the hours or days that follow.

Just like we remember who was the first president (Washington), the first man to walk on the moon (Armstrong), and the first person to fly across the Atlantic (Lindbergh), but we don't remember who was the second (Adams, Aldrin, and Earhart), we are less impacted by the second meeting with a person than by the first one. *You never get a second chance to make a first impression.*

Make sure you make a **good** first impression on a team member in the first interaction.

Habit #37: Time

Don't monopolize time

Extroverts, confident people, leaders, and public speakers like to talk...

But when you speak, you can't learn anything you didn't already know. You don't get a chance to learn what others are thinking, different perspectives on the topic, or if the others even understand what you say.

Make sure you let others speak. One of the ground rules I typically put forth at the beginning of a meeting is to not let anyone monopolize the "airtime." If you are the meeting leader or facilitator—make sure you stop people from monopolizing the meeting.

But most important, make sure you are not doing it yourself, even if you still have something to say. Make sure you don't take more than your fair share of the meeting time.

Oh, and you don't get to determine what's fair...

Get your butt out of your office

As Albert Mehrabian found in his 1960s research (published in *Silent Messages* in 1971), our likability by other people relies 7% on the words we use, 38% on our tone of voice, and 55% on our body language. The same can be said about trust. To build trust, you must increase the intimacy level of communications with your teammates.

You would not become trustworthy based on email messages (especially bulk, impersonal messages). You have a better chance of becoming trusted by your teammates if you speak with them over the phone.

But they will trust you the most when they see your body language as well. Do your best to meet with your teammates face-to-face. Get your butt out of your office. True team and trust building happen in face-to-face meetings.

And you could probably use the exercise…

Body language of email and text

Some communications would still have to take place over email or text messages.

Those contain body language as well. I know, sounds crazy, right? But while not amounting to the 38% conveyed through tone of voice, or the 55% through body language, you could still convey more than 7% of what you really mean through the body language of email.

You can achieve that through things like:

The opening (Hi, Dear,...), salutation (Mr., Ms., Dr., ...), using their name (spelled correctly...), the actual words you use in the email, using ALL CAPITALS (angry), punctuation (???, !!!, ...), emojis and emoticons (😊, 🙁, ...), being brief (may indicating annoyance) or verbose (happiness), formal or precise language (commanding), and more.

You can still convey a lot between your typed words and lines.

Habit #40: Intimacy

Own your side of communications

When you communicate **to** a teammate (any person, really), there is a message forming in your brain, which is turned into words through your mouth, and through their ears back into a message in their brain. This happens in the other direction as well.

Often, the original message generated in one brain is not the same as the final message understood by the other. Whose fault is that?

Probably both of you. The first person didn't communicate it clearly, and the recipient didn't understand it correctly.

"You didn't understand what I said," or "You didn't explain it well" are assigning the blame to the other side, putting them on the defense.

"I didn't explain it well," and "I'm not sure I understood" is owning your side of the communication and increasing your trustworthiness.

Habit #41: Intimacy

Be vulnerable

The dictionary defines vulnerability as *"the quality or state of being exposed to the possibility of being attacked or harmed, either physically or emotionally."*

Your vulnerability during an interaction with a team member is your willingness to expose yourself to them. Not inappropriately...

It's your willingness to share intimate things (again, appropriate) about yourself that, if your teammate wanted to, could be later used against you.

Vulnerability is often reciprocal. When the other person sees that you are willing to be vulnerable with them, most likely they will trust you enough to be vulnerable with you. After all, they will be less worried that you might abuse their vulnerability because you exposed your own vulnerability to be abused by them, and you showed them that you trust them.

Don't abuse your teammates' vulnerability

If you allow yourself to be vulnerable with your teammates, odds are that they will reciprocate and be willing to be vulnerable with you. They might even allow themselves to be vulnerable with you **before** you do that.

Either way, don't make them regret being vulnerable with you.

If they tell you a personal story of hardship, this would not be the time to put them down.

If they tell you a story of failure, making fun of them would not be an appropriate response.

If they show you a weakness, showing them that you are stronger will not make them feel better about themselves, or about being vulnerable with you, or trust you.

If your teammates are willing to be vulnerable with you, they are trusting you. Don't abuse it.

Respect teammates' boundaries

We all have boundaries. You have your own boundaries, and so do your teammates.

The boundaries could be in the form of off-the-table topics. If you feel that your teammate is not willing to talk about something, don't push.

Those boundaries could be reasonable or unreasonable (in your opinion). But remember that they are always reasonable to **them**. Don't force an issue you feel that your teammate is not willing to discuss.

The boundaries could even be physical. Some people need a bigger physical space than others. Give them that space and get out of their face.

Make sure that you are sensitive enough to observe your teammates' boundaries, and never violate them.

Don't be silent in meetings

Introverts don't particularly like to speak in meetings. Some people prefer to listen to others before voicing their own opinions.

That's OK, but when you don't speak in a meeting, others cannot learn from you, may have a feeling that you are not contributing, and generally will not develop trust in you. Remember that trust gets built with interactions, and if you are silent in a meeting—you are not interacting.

One of the ground rules I use in meetings is to never allow anyone to be silent during a meeting.

Even if nobody has established this ground rule for your team or for this specific meeting, don't be silent during the meeting. Speak, animate, interact. Let your teammates build trust in you.

Habit #45: Intimacy

Civilian Life

The Navy *Blue Angels* fly F/A-18 Hornets (my favorite fighter jet ever) 18" from wingtip-to-wingtip. The level of trust required to perform such maneuvers is one that you might never experience throughout your entire life.

Blue Angels pilots have a two-year rotation, and every year a few new pilots will be joining the team. Can they be trusted?

One of the final tests the candidates (typically 15 of them) will go through is the **social setting** test. The new pilots are invited to an outing with the families.

There is a lot that you can learn about a person when they are outside of their normal, professional setting.

The same applies to you. Do things with your team outside of work. Let them see who you are in "civilian life," and learn who *they* are.

Habit #46: Intimacy

Don't be politically correct, but don't be a jackass either

Political Correctness (PC) is a loaded subject. Heck, I wrote a whole book about it. Some confuse PC with politeness and respect.

To me, PC is saying something you don't mean, just to avoid a conflict or a meaningful discussion, and for fear of the possible negative feelings that could arise from it. Someone is politically correct when they tell you what you want to hear instead of what they really mean/feel. But they will tell others what they really think. Just not in front of you.

You can sense when someone is being politically correct with you. So can your teammates.

Don't be politically correct. Say what you mean and feel. Have the discussion. But that doesn't give you a license to be disrespectful. Those are two completely different things.

Say what you mean, mean what you say

Remember Albert Mehrabian? 7% of what you mean is conveyed through your **Words**, 38% through your **Tone** of voice, and 55% through your **Facial** expressions (can you create an acronym for that?)

What do you think you have the **least** conscious control over? That's right—your body language and facial expressions. The same things that convey the **most** of your message and intentions. On the other hand, you have the **most** conscious control over the words you say, even though they have the **least** effect on the listener.

So, if you say one thing and mean another, your teammates would know. Big time.

If you say what you mean and mean what you say, your teammates will trust you.

Habit #48: Intimacy

Watch your tone and body language

If 55% of your message is conveyed through your body language, and 38% through your tone of voice, shouldn't you pay more attention to those than to the words you use?

Some of those you can't control. In fact, you have less conscious control over your body language (followed by your tone of voice) than you do over the words that you use.

But some of those you can control. Watch what you wear, how you carry your notebook, briefcase, what your car looks like, etc.

Watch how you stand (or sit) in front of another employee. Get your feet off the table, even if you are the most senior person on the team. Watch how you speak.

Practice, practice, practice. You don't want to send the wrong message.

Habit #49: Intimacy

Watch your teammate's tone and body language

Guess what? The 7-38-55 rule works the other direction as well.

Don't just pay attention to the words that come out of your teammate's mouth. Pay attention to their tone and body language.

You already do this subconsciously. Why not train yourself to do it consciously, so you can learn not only what your teammate is telling you, but also what he or she is **not** telling you?

Don't put them on the spot, but if you feel they are not telling you what they really mean, consider saying something like: "I *hear* you, but I can *feel* that this is not exactly what you mean. Can you tell me what you *really* want to tell me?"

Don't push too hard. Let them feel comfortable telling you. Or not.

Admit to your flaws (but don't accept them)

When receiving feedback, admit to your flaws. Even if you don't think they are real, admit to the fact that this is the perception that you create.

It starts by admitting that you are not perfect. Admit to the flaws that you have.

However, don't accept those flaws ("this is who I am, take it or leave it.")

Yes, some flaws are incurable, but I would be surprised if your team will give you feedback about your asymmetrical eyebrows or that you limp. They won't.

The feedback that you receive, and the flaws you would hear about are most likely those which prevent trust and effective teamwork.

Commit to work on them, but take it one step at a time. Don't overcommit and underdeliver.

Habit #51: Positivity

Be a cheerleader

You can pour energy into a team meeting, but you can also suck the oxygen out of it.

In 2009, I was about to enter a customer meeting when I read an email from one of my PhD dissertation committee members. It started with "I don't think you are anywhere near ready to move on to the next stage of your research..."

Needless to say, I wasn't a cheerleader in that meeting... And I'm sure the customer noticed. The meeting probably could have gone so much better if I hadn't read that email right before it started.

My first advice is to never read emails not related to the meeting right before it starts...

But on a more serious note, your demeanor during the meeting can dramatically influence its outcome. Be a cheerleader, not a Debbie Downer.

Bottom line first or last?

If I want something from you, do you want me to tell you the "bottom line" first and only afterwards explain my rationale for what I want? Or do you want me to explain my thought process first, and only at the end give you the bottom line?

In a survey I conducted, I found that 74% of participants wanted to hear the bottom line first (I'm one of those), 17% wanted to hear the thought process first, leading to the bottom line at the end, and 9% would take it either way.

You may be different than your teammate in that preference. From my experience (with a prior colleague), if you are—this could lead to a reduced sense of shared values and trust.

The simple solution is: ask! "Do you want me to give you the bottom line first, or to explain how I got there first?"

Habit #53: Positivity

Say "I don't know"

What happens when a team member asks you a question to which you don't know the answer?

Do you make up an answer?

Do you ignore the question?

Don't! It doesn't matter if this happened publicly or during a one-on-one interaction.

Say "I don't know." Now, repeat after me: "I don't know." Now, go stand in front of a mirror and say, "I don't know."

It doesn't feel great to do that. I know. You may feel stupid. You may feel inadequate. You may worry that you might disappoint the team.

But you won't. You would show that you are human and willing to be vulnerable. And you are increasing your trustworthiness.

Promise to find the answer later, and do that.

Habit #54: Positivity

Say "I was wrong"

What do you do when a teammate calls you out on a mistake, or an incorrect statement that you made? Your reaction could define your trustworthiness as a member of the team.

If you get defensive and provide a flimsy explanation of why you were **not** wrong, and that under unique circumstances (that your team member will likely never encounter in his/her life) your statement would be true—you lose credibility and trustworthiness. They won't trust anything you say anymore.

Learn how to say, "I was wrong." After you mastered that statement, move on to the advanced level, and say "you were right."

But go even a step further. Even if your teammate did not catch your mistake, yet **you** did—admit to it anyway. Expect that he or she will catch it later, when you are no longer there to admit to it.

Say "It was my fault"

A friend got me into the radio-controlled airplane flying hobby a decade ago. Once, we flew out of a park behind his house. Upon takeoff, he crashed. He immediately blamed the wind, the grass we took off from, the battery, the motor, and anything else but...

Himself.

There is a very strong relationship between accountability and trust. We don't trust people who don't take ownership to their failures or their part in the team's failure.

You may only play a small part in the failure of the team, but if you don't recognize it and own it, you are destined to repeat your mistakes. And so would the team.

When something goes wrong, own your part of the failure and indicate so to the team. Don't let anyone at the team take the blame for your mistakes.

Habit #56: Positivity

Use empathy

Don't confuse empathy with sympathy, pity, or compassion. Those are completely different things.

Babies and cats have something in common: they both think that the world revolves around **them**.

As we grow up, though, we learn to "love thy neighbor as thyself," or do to your neighbor what you would like done to you. However, I love sushi and my wife can't stand it. Should I take her to eat sushi on **her** birthday because that's what **I** would like to do on mine? Bad idea.

Furthermore, we like to "put ourselves in other people's shoes." But you are not them.

Empathy is one of the most important qualities of a trustworthy team member. It is your ability to see things from your teammates' perspective, as if you were **them**. Not yourself.

Listen with intent

Stephen R. Covey said that "most people do not listen with the intent to **understand**; they listen with the intent to **reply**."

This varies with culture. In some cultures, people let you finish your sentence, then they think about what you said, and only then provide a thoughtful response. Some would start responding before you finish speaking. Heck, I come from a culture where you would be lucky to be able to squeeze in a word...

To be considered a trustworthy team member, listen carefully when your teammates speak. Listen to **what** they say, and note **how** they say it. Pay attention not only to what was said, but also to what was **not** said.

Don't start answering and don't start developing your answer before they are done talking, but rather seek to understand. It's OK to ask clarifying questions before you answer.

Habit #58: Positivity

If something bothers you, say it!

If something is not going the way you believe it should, and you don't say anything, you begin to harbor negative feelings towards another teammate. Eventually, this will blow out of proportion, and you might take it out on your teammate in a much worse way than if you said something when it started bothering you.

Your teammates can't read your mind. We've established that already. They may not know what is bothering you, but trust you me—they will know that something is bothering you. Your body language will tell them, and you can't control that. They may assume that something else is bothering you, if you don't tell them.

If something bothers you, say something. Have the discussion. Maybe it's something easy to change. Maybe not, but at least you address it, and everyone know where they stand.

Habit #59: Positivity

Give direct and honest feedback

When a teammate does something wrong, give them direct and honest feedback. Don't sugar-coat it. No need to be mean when you do it, either. You don't want to push them to be defensive. Deliver feedback in a way that demonstrates that you have their best interest in mind.

In your feedback, focus on actions and behaviors and not on personalities. Once you have trust, you should be able to say, "that was a stupid idea," but you should never say "you're stupid." The first will be received positively. The second will be received negatively.

Your teammate will sense when you give a positive feedback that you don't really mean. Remember that you have the least conscious control over your body language, which will convey what you really mean the most.

Know how much feedback is right

You can give too much feedback, and if you do, you might put the recipient of that feedback on the defense, forcing him/her to become emotional, and therefore irrational.

The more trust there is between you and your teammate, the more direct your feedback may be, without them being offended by it.

On the other hand, giving direct and honest feedback increases trust. So, what's the right thing to do?

Think of the correlation between the level of feedback you can use with your teammate and the level of trust between the two of you as positively linear.

If you provide less feedback than appropriate to that level of trust, you may increase trust. But if you provide more than appropriate—you may destroy it.

Habit #61: Positivity

The right time and place for feedback

"There is a time for everything, and a season for every activity under the heavens."

- Ecclesiastes 3

Think about the setting for providing feedback. This about the **time**, the **place**, and the **audience**.

If the person you want to give feedback to is not in "listening mode," maybe this is not the time. Maybe your teammate is in a hurry. Maybe they are having a bad day already. Maybe they are about to do something that requires significant concentration and your feedback has nothing to do with it, yet could distract them.

Public shaming is not feedback. When you give personal feedback, do it personally with nobody else present.

Habit #62: Positivity

Ask for feedback and be receptive to it

You are not perfect. Hopefully I'm not telling you anything you didn't already know. However, sometimes you don't even know what is it that you are doing wrong.

Ask your teammates for feedback. You must be genuine when you ask for it, and the best way to do that is by really **wanting** to get that feedback, so you can improve. At least your trustworthiness.

Know that even if only 10% of what you hear is true, 100% is true in **perception**. If the perception that your teammates have is not what you want them to have, that's on you. You are doing something wrong.

Your teammates will initially hesitate from giving you feedback. Over time, if they see that you are receptive to it and improve, you will get more feedback. Be patient.

Habit #63: Positivity

Reduce your own sensitivity— don't get defensive

So, you asked your teammates for feedback, and they gave it to you. Big time. They might say something to you that would hurt your feelings. If they do, they will likely say it without the **intention** of hurting you. Nevertheless, it would still be hurtful to you.

You have two options: you can become defensive (and act like it), or you can reduce your sensitivity and learn and benefit from it. Remember, if your teammates didn't intend to hurt you, the decision to get hurt, defensive, emotional, and irrational is completely **yours**. With very little benefit.

Frankly, even if they **did** intend to hurt your feelings, the decision whether to get defensive and emotional is yours, still with little benefit.

If you can take the feedback, as hurtful as it might be, with stride—you will show receptivity.

If you can't take feedback now, say it

A teammate of yours is coming to give you feedback (not a positive one). However, as much as you would like to reduce your sensitivity and not be defensive, this is simply not the right time or place for you to take this feedback.

You may be distraught, you may be about to start something that requires your 100% concentration, or there are other people around, and you prefer to take this feedback privately, at the right time.

Just like I asked you to give your teammate feedback at the right time and place, your teammate should do the same.

But he/she may not know this is not the right time. Tell them. Suggest another time and follow up. You need this feedback, but you need to take it when you are receptive to it.

Be humble

Arrogance always leaves a bad impression. You may be the smartest person in the room, but you shouldn't be flaunting it around.

Arrogance might also prevent you from listening to your team members or giving any weight to their opinions, killing vulnerability, feedback, and receptivity all at the same time.

Humility starts inside you. You must first accept that you may not be the smartest person in the room, to start listening to others.

Humility doesn't end with words. Remember that you have the least conscious control over your body language, yet your body language carries most of your intention and meaning.

If you choose your words carefully to show humility while your body language suggests the opposite, your teammates will see you as arrogant and insincere.

Bad is 3 times stronger than good

The following companies have less than 2-star customer review scores (out of 5 stars, when the lowest rating you can give is 1 star) with the Better Business Bureau (BBB): Amazon, Southwest Airlines, Google, Apple, and Ford.

Why is that?

Several theories, including the *Prospect Theory* (which won its authors the Nobel Prize), the *Critical Positivity Ratio* (also known as the *Losada Ratio*), and others, showed that people respond three times stronger to a negative event than to a positive one. We are three times more likely to post a negative review than a positive one.

Every bad behavior (by you) in an interaction will take three positive behaviors in following meetings just to break even.

Focus more on doing less bad and less on doing more good.

Habit #67: Positivity

Humor/sarcasm when appropriate

Research showed that humor and sarcasm could be catalysts for creativity, productivity, and overall positivity. However, a *Harvard University* study also showed that those positive effects could only occur in the presence of **trust**. When trust doesn't exist, the use of humor and sarcasm can lead to conflict instead.

It's just like providing feedback. There is a linear relationship between the level of trust that already exists and the level of humor and sarcasm you can use without destroying trust.

When you feel you have established enough trust, start using those to develop a positive relationship and accelerate trust. But tread carefully, because you don't want to overdo it. Err on the side of caution, and remember: bad is still three times stronger than good.

And remember this, too: what's funny for you may not be funny to the other person.

Habit +1

Know when to give up

Not 100% of your team members will trust you, even if you implemented everything in this book, even if you are more trustworthy than any other person in the organization.

First, remember that the level of trust you get from a teammate is the product of *their* **trustability** (willingness to trust **anyone**) and *your* **trustworthiness**. Maybe the issue is not your trustworthiness, but really their trustability.

Maybe it's not them. Maybe it *is* you. There is just something about you that doesn't work with that specific team member. Remember trust law #3: trust exists independently between two people. Just not between the two of you.

For example, you don't share the same values. That doesn't make either of you wrong. You are simply not on the same page. Maybe you both hold strong opposing political positions, maybe you are both very passionate about those positions, and just can't separate them from your professional relationship.

Don't pretend to change your political affiliation. Don't pretend to change which football team you like (or whether you like football at all) just to **fake** shared values.

You must know when to give up. Maybe you just can't build trust with that team member.

If they don't trust you, you will not be able to hold constructive disagreements with them, and instead have disagreement that are politically correct, destructive, and anything but effective, creative, or productive.

You will not trust them, and in return, they will not behave in a trustworthy way. And vice versa.

However, if you can't build trust with that team member, **you should not be working together**. You will not be doing yourself or the other member any favor by trying to work together. Go to your leader and ask for one of you to be reassigned out of the team.

Finally, remember the words of Tacitus:

"He that fights and runs away, may turn and fight another day; But he that is in battle slain, will never rise to fight again."

About the Author

Dr. Yoram Solomon is the founder of the Innovation Culture Institute, LLC. He published 11 books, 22 patents, more than 200 articles, and was one of the creators of Wi-Fi and  USB 3.0 technologies. Named one of the Top 40 Innovation Bloggers in 2015, 2016, 2017, and 2018, top 20 Global Though Leaders on Culture, and was a columnist at Inc. Magazine, Innovation Excellence, and other publications.

He founded several startups and sold one of them in Silicon Valley. He worked at different roles from General Manager of a $100m business unit in a Fortune 200 company to a Vice President of Corporate Strategy and Innovation, and CEO.

Dr. Solomon is an adjunct Professor of entrepreneurship and innovation at the Southern Methodist University, the University of Texas at Dallas, and the Hadassah Academic College in Jerusalem. In 2015 he was elected to the Plano Independent School District board.

He is a professional speaker at the National Speakers Association, and a **TEDx** speaker and host.

Yoram brings his experience as a marksman, serving in the IDF 35th Airborne Paratrooper brigade, and as a USAF CAP pilot.

About ICI

Originally, the Innovation Culture Institute LLC was formed in 2005 to help companies innovate. Founded by innovator and entrepreneur Dr. Yoram Solomon, its initial mission was to help companies at any size generate ideas.

However, through his research, Dr. Solomon found that companies could not innovate if they didn't first have a **culture of innovation**. Furthermore, he found that a culture of innovation could not exist before those companies had high levels of **trust**.

This is when he developed the **trustactions**™ model and formula set, based on original research, and work done with many clients.

Today, the Institute helps companies and organizations increase the level of trust they have, the level of trust the public and community has in them, and helps individuals (leaders, team members, sales people, politicians, and many more) increase their level of trustworthiness.

We do that through inspiring keynotes, interactive in-depth workshops, assessments, coaching, training, and consulting.

To find out more, check our website, **www.innovationcultureinstitute.com**, call us at **(972) 332-1490**, or text **TRUST** to **21000**.

 Innovation Culture Institute

Other Resources

Additional Books by Yoram Solomon:

Culture starts with YOU, not your boss!

Un-Kill Creativity

Blueprints for the Next Big Thing

Bowling with a Crystal Ball (2nd Ed.)

From Startup to Maturity

Business Plan through Investors' Eyes

Worst Diet Ever

Cause of Death: Political Correctness

For more information, links, free downloads and resources:

Or text **TRUST** to **21000**

More books in this series

Habits that will make you a trustworthy—

- ❖ Salesperson
- ❖ Leader
- ❖ Team member
- ❖ Human Resources professional
- ❖ Consultant
- ❖ Educator
- ❖ Politician
- ❖ Financial Advisor
- ❖ Realtor
- ❖ Negotiator
- ❖ Entrepreneur
- ❖ Child (children's book)
- ❖ Brand
- ❖ Spouse
- ❖ Job Candidate

*Note: 67+1 habits that will make you a trustworthy **team member** is the third book in the series, and others may not yet be available at the time you are reading this book.*

Made in the USA
Columbia, SC
04 July 2019